Penguin Modern European Poets
Advisory Editor: A. Alvarez

Selected Poems - Yehuda Amichai

Yehuda Amichai was born in 1924 in Würzbürg,
Germany, but when he was thirteen his family moved
to Jerusalem. His first book appeared in 1955. Since then
he has published four other volumes of poetry and one
of short stories. His novel *Not of This Time, Not of This
Place* has been published in Israel and the United States.
Amichai is regarded as one of the leading writers of
post-war Israel. His poetry and prose have been awarded
the Shlonsky Prize and two Acum Prizes, and his play
Bells and Trains won the first prize in Kol, the country's
competition for original radio plays. He now lives by
teaching in Jerusalem, and is a sergeant-major in the
Israeli army. He was visiting poet at the University of
Berkeley, California, during the autumn of 1971. He is
married and has one son.

Selected Poems

Yehuda Amichai

Translated by
Assia Gutmann and
Harold Schimmel with
the collaboration of
Ted Hughes

With an Introduction by
Michael Hamburger

Penguin Books

Penguin Books Ltd, Harmondsworth,
Middlesex, England
Penguin Books Australia Ltd, Ringwood,
Victoria, Australia

This selection first published 1971
Copyright © Yehuda Amichai, 1968, 1971
Translations copyright © Celia Chaikin, 1968, 1971;
© Harold Schimmel, 1971
Introduction copyright © Michael Hamburger, 1968,
1971

The following translations, by Assia Gutmann, are taken
from *Yehuda Amichai: Selected Poems,* published by Cape
Goliard, 1968: 'Ibn Gabirol', 'My Parents' Migration',
'King Saul and I', 'Out of Three or Four in a Room',
'My Father Fought Their War for Four Years', 'The
United Nations Command in Jerusalem', 'Farewell
You', 'It Was Summer, or the End of Summer',
'Mayor', 'God Has Pity on Kindergarten Children',
'To My Mother', 'As for the World', 'Like Our
Bodies' Imprint', 'Two Quatrains', 'A Pity. We Were
Such a Good Invention', 'If with a Bitter Mouth',
'The Place Where I've Not Been', 'Two Songs on
Caesaria Beach', 'You Also Were So Tired', and 'In the
Middle of This Century'.

Made and printed in Great Britain by
C. Nicholls & Company Ltd
Set in Monotype Garamond

Contents

Introduction

When it was proposed that I write an introduction to Yehuda Amichai's poems my first impulse was to refuse. Poems are made of words, and I cannot read the words of which Amichai's poems are made, cannot follow – let alone judge – his way with the Hebrew language, what he does with its ancient and modern, literary and vernacular components, how he combines and contrasts them to make them talk or sing as they have never talked or sung before. I had heard Amichai read in London and had both heard and read some of his poems in translation. Something about his relation to the language in which he writes could be gathered from the poem 'National Thoughts', where it is characterized as

          this tired language
Torn from its sleep in the Bible, –
Blinded, it lurches from mouth to mouth, –
The language which described God and the Miracles,
Says:
Motor car, bomb, God.

The relation is not a simple one, because Amichai cannot take his language for granted. For one thing, it was not his first language; and the language itself is an historical anomaly, like other languages that have not grown continuously and organically, but have been preserved, revived and modernized with a high degree of deliberateness. Amichai's awareness of that peculiarity is inseparable from the historical awareness that distinguishes all his work. The repetition of 'God' in the sixth line of the passage quoted is seemingly contrary to the logic and rhetoric of argument. It sets up an ironic tension between the deity worshipped in Biblical times and the purposes which the old religion can be made to serve in the age of motor cars and bombs. Amichai, therefore, is not only characterizing a language, but rendering the predicament of those who use it; and the rendering includes a criticism.

The background of Amichai's poems is almost as unfamiliar to me as their language. Almost. For though I have never seen Israel, and was not brought up within the rites and traditions of Judaism, Amichai is a first-generation Palestinian, born in the same country, Germany, and in the same year, 1924, as myself. Amichai's first language was German, and it has been suggested that his way with the Hebrew language owes much to that circumstance. The biographical link in itself may seem tenuous enough, but the more I immersed myself in Amichai's poems and in his novel, *Not of This Time, Not of This Place,** the less tenuous it became for me.

If in 1936 Amichai's family had emigrated not to Palestine but to Britain or America, he would have written in English, as I do, or in German, as his near-coevals Paul Celan and Erich Fried continued to do, though one lived in Paris, the other lives in London. The fact that Amichai's parents were Jewish enough to choose Palestine, and to send their son to a Jewish school before their emigration, is far from being irrelevant to the poems. But neither is Amichai's pervasive awareness of what he owes to the Diaspora, his sense of displacement, anachronism, division, incongruousness, fortuitousness, his ironic shifts between three layers of Jewish history – the Biblical past, the new
*Harper & Row, New York, 1967.

nation's future and, separating these two, the long, unheroic, wearying centuries of dispersion, terminated by the destruction of Jewish communities throughout the greater part of Europe. Not only is Amichai's novel set both in Jerusalem and in his native South Germany, but the alternating chapters of first and third person narrative convey the simultaneous presence of one character in both settings. Only this extreme resort enabled Amichai to give his novel the full dimensions of his own awareness; and whatever the themes of his poems, the same multiple awareness informs them all.

In the collection *The Hebrew Poem Itself** I found transliterations of the Hebrew texts of four poems by Amichai, together with literal renderings and critical analyses of the same poems. These not only confirmed that Amichai's poems show the influence of modern English and German poets, but revealed that the poem rendered here as 'My Father Fought Their War for Four Years' was written as a sonnet, with a rhyme scheme basically Shakespearean, and that the title and refrain of another poem are derived from a phrase in a lease contract – a phrase to which Amichai gives implications and modulations of meaning undreamt of in the legal profession. One of his Hebrew texts contains the words 'Luna Park' – a loan word derived from German fairgrounds and amusement centres with that name, but used by Amichai in such a way as to invoke distinct childhood associations with the German prototype. What another critic† has censured as 'mere metaphorical fireworks' in some of Amichai's

*Holt, Rinehart & Winston, New York, 1965, pp. 160–67.

†Arieh Sachs, 'The Poetry of Yehuda Amichai', in *Judaism*, Vol. 14, No. 4, 1965, p. 409.

poems strikes me as a resort analogous to the simultaneity rendered by the narrative structure of his novel: seemingly incompatible images are juxtaposed or telescoped in order to enact Amichai's essential awareness of simultaneity. If that awareness is essential to Amichai's work the same critic is wrong to speak of 'shock tactics' or of 'a kind of superabundance, sometimes overabundance' in his works, 'a feeling (sic) that the richness of the metaphorical display sometimes exceeds the emotional matter with which it is designed to deal'. If the emotional matter of a poem has not been fully enacted within that poem, we have no means of knowing what it was; and in Assia Gutmann's translations, at any rate, the metaphors do their job of relating and contrasting the everyday with the mythical, heroic and exemplary, the poet's own experience with that of Biblical or mediaeval paradigms, King Saul or Ibn Gabirol.

It is his acute historical consciousness that makes Amichai's poems at once tragic and humorous, tender and tough, direct and intricate. Although he has fought in two wars, against the Germans and against the Arabs, he cannot accept the simplifications of nationalism. Although he is steeped in Jewish scripture, he cannot accept the certainties of an exclusive faith. For Amichai, therefore, to be an Israeli is quite as difficult as to be a Diaspora Jew; and his preoccupation with his parents, in the poems, means that he assumes the burdens and dilemmas of both. If it was imperative for Diaspora Jews to remember Jerusalem, the Kings and Prophets, his poems suggest, it is equally imperative for Israeli Jews to remember the Diaspora. Otherwise they will lose the benefits, as well as the scars, of a unique experience; and Israel will fall into the errors of other new nations, only more deeply and dangerously, because the threats and the desperation are greater. Amichai does not preach or prophesy; but his ironies and his gift of total recall provide a corrective to every kind of national complacency and intransigence. His sensibility remains European enough to experience the very landscape of Israel as savage and alien, as in the poem 'Mayor'; and he has retained the scepticism, liberalism and individualism which more militant Israeli intellectuals have been eager to discard. In the novel, too, the narrator-protagonist's plans for vengeance are thwarted by the complexities of human nature; and, as in the poems, no motive proves more powerful or more tenacious than love, a love sharpened by the awareness of pain, transitiveness and death.

Many of Amichai's poems are intimately personal without being mere private confessions. Just as he applies a long historical memory to the immediate situation of his country, he applies a sense of his whole past life to any personal occasion. The questions he asks about his own life are also questions about other people's lives. His poem 'My Child', for instance, is also a poem about his father, about himself and about anyone. Although he is a poet of experience, rather than of innocence, his sense of history and alienation through history has not blunted his sense of wonder, any more than his 'tiredness' has impaired the energy of his poems. For all his knowingness, his perceptions are fresh. To read these poems, therefore, is both to be reminded of things one has tended to forget and to discover things that one has never known.

MICHAEL HAMBURGER

Translated by Assia Gutmann

King Saul and I

1

They gave him a finger, but he took the whole hand
They gave me the whole hand: I didn't even take the
  little finger.
While my heart
Was weightlifting its first feelings
He rehearsed the tearing of oxen.

My pulse-beats were like
Drips from a tap
His pulse-beats
Pounded like hammers on a new building.

He was my big brother
I got his used clothes.

2

His head, like a compass, will always bring him
To the sure north of his future.

His heart is set, like an alarm clock
For the hour of his reign.
When everyone's asleep, he will cry out
Until all the quarries are hoarse.
Nobody will stop him!

Only the asses bare their yellow teeth
At the end.

3

Dead prophets turned time-wheels

When he went out searching for asses
Which I, now, have found.
But I don't know how to handle them.
They kick me.

I was raised with the straw,
I fell with heavy seeds.
But he breathed the winds of his histories.
He was anointed with the royal oil
As with wrestler's grease.
He battled with olive-trees
Forcing them to kneel.

Roots bulged on the earth's forehead
With the strain.
The prophets escaped from the arena;
Only God remained, counting:
Seven . . . eight . . . nine . . . ten . . .
The people, from his shoulders downwards, rejoiced.
Not a man stood up.
He had won.

4

I am tired,
My bed is my kingdom.

My sleep is just
My dream is my verdict.

I hung my clothes on a chair
For tomorrow.

He hung his kingdom
In a frame of golden wrath
On the sky's wall.

My arms are short, like string too short
To tie a parcel.

His arms are like the chains in a harbour
For cargo to be carried across time.

He is a dead king.
I am a tired man.

Ibn Gabirol

Sometimes pus
Sometimes a poem.

Something always bursts out.
And always pain.

My father was a tree in a forest of fathers
Covered in green cotton wool.

Oh, widows of the flesh, orphans of the blood,
I must escape.

Eyes sharp as tin-openers
Opened heavy secrets.

But through the wound on my chest
God peers into the world.

I am the door
To his apartment.

The Place Where I've Not Been

The place where I have not been
I never shall be.
The place where I have been
Is as though I have never been there. People stray
Far from the places where they were born
And far from the words which were spoken
As if by their mouths
And still wide of the promise
Which they were promised.

And they eat standing and die sitting
And lying down they remember.
And what I shall never in the world return to
And look at, I am to love for ever.
Only a stranger will return to my place. But I will set
    down
All these things once more, as Moses did,

After he smashed the first tablets.

Out of Three or Four in a Room

Out of three or four in a room
One is always standing at the window.
Forced to see the injustice amongst the thorns,
The fires on the hill.

And people who left whole
Are brought home in the evening, like small change.

Out of three or four in a room
One is always standing at the window.
Hair dark above his thoughts.
Behind him, the words.
And in front of him the words, wandering, without
    luggage.
Hearts without provision, prophecies without water
And big stones put there
And staying, closed, like letters
With no addresses; and no one to receive them.

If With a Bitter Mouth

If with a bitter mouth you will speak
Sweet words, the world will
Neither sweeten nor become more bitter.

And it is written in the book that we shall not fear.
And it is also written, that we shall change,
Like the words,
In future and in past,
Plural or alone.

And soon in the coming nights,
We shall appear, like strolling players
Each in the other's dream.

And into these dreams
There shall also come strangers
We did not know together.

In My Time, In Your Place

We were together in my time, in your place.
You gave the place and I the time.
Quietly your body waited for the seasons to change.
Fashions passed over it, to shorten, to lengthen,
With flowers or in white silk, clinging.

We swapped human values for those of beasts,
Calm and tiger-like and for ever.
And for all that, ready to burn any moment
With the dry grass of the end of summer.

I divided the days with you, nights.
We exchanged a look with rain,
I was your Lent and your Mardi Gras
In one body. We were not like dreamers,
Even in our dreams.

And in the unquiet, nestled the quiet,
In my time, in your place.

The many dreams I now dream of you
Prophesy your end with me –

As the multiplying crowds of seagulls
Come where the sea ends.

In My Worst Dreams

In my worst dreams
You, with bright eyes,
Are always standing near walls
Whose foundation stone
Is a heart.

Of all the things I do,
Parting is the inevitable one.

In my dreams I always hear a voice –
It is not my voice –
And not yours,
Neither is it the daughter of your voice.

Eyes creased, my eyes are
Like the eyes of exhausted beasts
Lusting for days
That have passed with the nights.

They have taken a love-mask off me
Just as they take a death-mask.
They took it without my noticing
As I lay beside you.

It is my true face.

Farewell You

Farewell you, your Face, already the Face of memory,
Wandering, rising from the world of the dead;
    and flying, flying.
Face of beasts, Face of water, Face of going,
 And a forest of whispers
Face of the womb, Face of child.

No longer ours the hours of touch,
No longer ours to say: Now, Now.
Yours was the name of winds, once the wife
Of directions, purpose, mirror and autumn.

Whatever we failed to understand, we sang
Together.
Generations and the dark, Face of alternation.
No longer mine, unsolved,
Locked nipples, buckles, mouths, screws.

Farewell then, you, the never sleeping
All was fulfilled by our word; that all is of sand.
From now on
Dream through your own dreams, the world and all.

Go in peace, go, bundles and cases of death.
Threads, feathers, the household mash, pawn of hair,
Whatever will not be, no hand writes,
Whatever was not of the body, will leave no memory.

A Pity. We Were Such a
Good Invention

They amputated
Your thighs off my hips.
As far as I'm concerned
They are all surgeons. All of them.

They dismantled us
Each from the other.
As far as I'm concerned
They are all engineers. All of them.

A pity. We were such a good
And loving invention.
An aeroplane made from a man and wife.
Wings and everything.
We hovered a little above the earth.

We even flew a little.

It Was Summer, or the
End of Summer

It was summer, or the end of summer
And I heard then your footsteps, as you went from
   east to west
For the last time. And in the world
Handkerchiefs were lost, and books, and people.

It was summer or the end of summer
There were hours in the afternoon,
You were;
And you wore your shroud
For the first time.
And you never noticed
Because it was embroidered with flowers.

Two Songs on Caesaria Beach

1

The sea preserves in salt.
Jerusalem preserves in dryness.
And where shall we go?
Now, in the exacting twilight,
To choose.
Not what we shall do
Or how we shall live
But to choose the life
Whose dreams
Will hurt least
In all the nights to come.

2

'Come again next summer,'
Or words like that
Hold my life
Take away my days
Like a line of soldiers
Passing over a bridge
Marked for exploding.
'Come again next summer,'

Who hasn't heard these words?

But who comes again?

Like Our Bodies' Imprint

Like our bodies' imprint
Not a sign will remain that we were in this place
The world closes behind us,
The sand straightens itself.

Dates are already in view
In which you no longer exist,
Already a wind blows clouds
Which will not rain on us both.

And your name is already in the passenger lists of ships
And in the registers of hotels,
Whose names alone
Deaden the heart.

The three languages I know,
All the colours in which I see and dream:

None will help me.

God Has Pity on
Kindergarten Children

God has pity on children in kindergartens,
He pities school children – less.
But adults he pities not at all.

He abandons them,
And sometimes they have to crawl on all fours
In the roasting sand
To reach the dressing station,
And they are streaming with blood.

But perhaps
He will have pity on those who love truly
And take care of them
And shade them
Like a tree over the sleeper on the public bench.

Perhaps even we will spend on them
Our last pennies of kindness
Inherited from mother,

So that their own happiness will protect us
Now and on other days.

Two Quatrains

1

Once I escaped, but I do not remember why or from
    which God,
I shall therefore travel through my life like Jonah in
    his dark fish,
We've settled it between us, I and the fish, we're both
    in the world's bowels,
I shall not come out, he will not digest me.

2

The last rains came on a warm night. In the morning
    my disaster blossomed.
The race is over. Who is first, who second?
After our death we could play: I shall be you, you – me
In the dead moon, in the dead moon, in the returning
    ancient time, in my window's tree.

Eye Examination

Go back a bit. Close your left eye.
Still?
Go back a bit further. The wall has moved on.
What do you see?
What do you recognize in the dimness?
I remember a lovely song which went . . .
Now? What do you see now?
Still? – All the time.
Don't leave me. Please. Please.
You're not leaving.
I'm not.
Close one eye. Speak in a loud voice.
I can't hear – I'm already far away.
What do you recognize? What do you see?

Close one sad eye.
Yes.
Close the other sad eye. Yes.
I can see now.

And nothing else.

In the Middle of This Century

In the middle of this century we turned to each other
With half faces and full eyes
Like an ancient Egyptian picture
And for a short while.

I stroked your hair
In the opposite direction to your journey,
We called to each other,
Like calling out the names of towns
Where nobody stops
Along the route.

Lovely is the world rising early to evil,
Lovely is the world falling asleep to sin and pity,
In the mingling of ourselves, you and I,
Lovely is the world.

The earth drinks men and their loves
Like wine,
To forget.
It can't.
And like the contours of the Judean hills,
We shall never find peace.

In the middle of this century we turned to each other,
I saw your body, throwing shade, waiting for me,
The leather straps for a long journey
Already tightening across my chest.
I spoke in praise of your mortal hips,
You spoke in praise of my passing face,

I stroked your hair in the direction of your journey,
I touched your flesh, prophet of your end,
I touched your hand which has never slept,
I touched your mouth which may yet sing.

Dust from the desert covered the table
At which we did not eat.
But with my finger I wrote on it
The letters of your name.

Poem in an Orange Grove

I am abandoned by God. 'You're abandoned by God,'
Said my father.
God forgot me
So did he, later.

The scent of orange groves in blossom
Was in me for a while. You. Hands sticky
With juice and love. You cried a great cry
And threw two of your last thighs into battle.
And then silence.
You, whose handsome head learnt history,
Know that only what's past is silent.
Even battles,
Even the scent of orange groves.
Blossoms and fruit were on one and the same tree,
Above us, in that double season.

Even then we spoke with that foreign
And strange accent of those who will die.

I Was the Moon

My child is very sad.

Whatever I teach him –
Geography of love
Strange languages which can't be heard
Because of the distance –
My child rocks his little bed towards me in the night
What am I?
More than forgetting.
The very language of forgotten.
And until he understands what I did
I am as good as dead.

What are you doing with our quiet child?
You cover him with a blanket
Like heaven, layers of clouds –
I could be the moon.

What are you doing with your sad fingers?
You dress them with gloves
And go out.

I was the moon.

As for the World

As for the world,
I am always like one of Socrates' disciples,
Walking by his side,
Hearing his opinions and histories
It remains for me to say:
Yes. Yes it is like that.
You are right again,
Indeed your words are true.

As for my life,
I am always like Venice:
Whatever is mere streets in others
Within me is a dark streaming love.

As for the cry, as for the silence,
I am always a *Shofar*:
All year hoarding its one blast
For the Terrible Days.

As for action
I am always like Cain:
Nomad
In the face of the act, which I will not do,
Or, having done,
Will make it irredeemable.

As for the palm of your hand,
As for the signals of my heart,
And the plans of my flesh,

As for the writing on the wall,
I am always ignorant,
I can neither read nor write
And my head is like the

Heads of those senseless weeds

Knowing only the rustle and drift
Of the wind
When a fate passes through me
To some other place.

She Knows

I know that she knows.
They think she doesn't, but know otherwise,
She knows.

My heart tears with this game
And in the night its blood hears the cry
Like the cry of paper tearing
Across the forty-two years of my life.

Under a broad vine,
In the yard of a house
In the Valley of Hinnom,
An old woman once told me:
'Because he was burnt inside,
His head turned white as snow.'
I forget what she was talking about
Or whom –
My life is forty-two years of torn paper.

Tourist

She showed me her swaying hair
In the four winds of her coming.
I showed her some of my folding ways of life
And the trick, and the lock.
She asked after my street and my house
And I laughed loudly.
She showed me this long night
And the interior of her thirty years.
I showed her the place where I once laid *tefillin*.

I brought her chapters and verses
And sand from Eilat
And the handing of the Torah
And the manna of my death
And all the miracles that have not yet healed in me.

She showed me the stages of joy
And my childhood's double.
I revealed to her that King David is not buried in
    his tomb
And that I don't live in my life.
While I was reflecting and she was eating,
The city map lay open on the table –
Her hand on Qatamon
My hand on hers –
The cup covered the Old City,
Ash dropped on the King David Hotel,
And an ancient weeping
Allowed us to lie together.

God's Fate

God's fate
Is now
The fate of trees rocks sun and moon,
The ones they stopped worshipping
When they began to believe in God.

But He's forced to remain with us
As are the trees, as are the rocks
Sun moon and stars.

My Mother Once Told Me

My mother once told me
Not to sleep with flowers in the room.
Since then I have not slept with flowers.
I sleep alone, without them.

There were many flowers.
But I've never had enough time.
And persons I love are already pushing themselves
Away from my life, like boats
Away from the shore.

My mother said
Not to sleep with flowers.
You won't sleep.
You won't sleep, mother of my childhood.

The bannister I clung to
When they dragged me off to school
Is long since burnt.
But my hands, clinging,
Remain
Clinging.

My Parents' Migration

And my parents' migration has not yet calmed in me.
My blood goes on shaking at its walls,
As the bowl after it is set down.
And my parents' migration has not yet calmed in me.
Winds continually over stones.
Earth forgets the footsteps of those who walk.
An awful fate. Stumps of talk after midnight.
An achievement, a retreat. Night reminds
And day forgets.
My eyes which have looked a long time into a vast
    desert,
Are a little calmed. One woman. The rules of a
    game
Nobody had ever completely explained. The laws of
    pain and weight.

Even now my heart
Makes only a bare living
With its daily love.
My parents in their migration.
On the crossroads where I am forever orphaned,
Too young to die, too old to play.
The weariness of the miner
The emptiness of the quarry
In one body.
Archaeology of the future
Museums of what is still to happen.
And my parents' migration has not yet calmed in me,
And from bitter peoples I learned bitter languages
For my silence among the houses

Which are always
Like ships.

Already my veins, my tendons
Are a tangle of ropes I will never undo
Finally, my own
Death
And an end to my parents' migration.

To Summon Witnesses

When did I last weep?
The time has come to summon witnesses.
Of those who last saw me weep
Some are dead.

I wash my eyes with a lot of water
So as to see the world once more
Through the wet and the hurt.

I must find witnesses.

Lately, I have felt for the first time
Needle stabs in my heart.
I am not frightened,
I am almost proud, like a boy
Who discovers the first hairs in his armpits
And between his legs.

The End of Elul*

I'm tired of summer.
The smoke rising from the convent of the silent nuns
Is all I have to say.
This year winter will come late
When we're ready for its coming,
And we won't be.

I'm tired. And curse the three Great Religions
Which won't let me sleep at night
What with bells and howls of muezzins and loud
 shofars and noisy atonements.
Oh God, close your houses, let the world rest.
Why hast thou *not* forsaken me?
This year the year hesitates.
The summer drags on.
If it weren't for the tears that I have kept back all
 these years,
I'd have dried up like thorns.

Great battles are conducted within me in dreadful
 quiet,
With only the sighs of thousands of sweating, naked
 wrestlers.
There is no iron, and no stone, only flesh, like snakes;
And afterwards, they'll fall away one from the other
 with surfeit and weakness,
And there'll be clouds, and there'll be rain
When we're ready for it, and we won't be.

* Elul is the last month of summer.

Quick and Bitter

The end was quick and bitter.
Slow and sweet was the time between us,
Slow and sweet were the nights
When my hands did not touch one another in despair
But with the love of your body
Which came between them.

And when I entered into you
It seemed then that great happiness
Could be measured with the precision
Of sharp pain. Quick and bitter.

Slow and sweet were the nights.
Now is as bitter and grinding as sand –
'We shall be sensible' and similar curses.

And as we stray further from love
We multiply the words,
Words and sentences long and orderly.
Had we remained together
We could have become a silence.

Luxury

My uncle is buried at Sheik Baadar.
The other one is scattered in the Carpathian mountains.

My father is buried in the Synhedria,
My grandmother on the Mount of Olives
And all their forefathers
Are buried in the ruined Jewish cemeteries in the
    villages of Lower Franconia,
Near rivers and forests which are not Jerusalem.

My father's father kept heavy-eyed
Jewish cows in their sheds below the kitchen –

And rose at four in the morning.
I inherited his early rising,
My mouth bitter with nightmares:
I attend to my bad dreams.

Grandfather, Grandfather,
Chief Rabbi of my life,
As you sold unleavened bread on the Passover Eve,
Sell my pains –
So they stay in me, even ache, but not mine,
Not my property.

So many tombstones are scattered behind me –
Names, engraved like the names of long-abandoned
    railway stations.
How shall I cover all these distances,
How can I keep them connected?
I can't afford such an intricate network.
It's a luxury.

Two Songs of Peace

1

My son smells of peace when I lean over him.
It isn't just the soap.
Everybody was once the child with the smell of peace.
(And in the whole country there isn't a single
    windmill which turns.)

Oh torn country, like torn clothes
Which can't be mended,
And hard, lonely forefathers in Hebron's grave
In childless silence.

My son smells of peace.
His mother's womb
Promised him that
Which God can't promise us.

2

My love was not in the war.
She learns love and history
Off my body, which was in two, or three.
And at night.
When my body makes battles into peace
She is bewildered.
Her perplexity is her love. And her learning.
Her wars and her peace, her dream.

And I am now in the middle of my life.
The time when one begins to collect
Facts, and many details,
And exact maps

Of a country we shall never occupy
And of an enemy and lover
Whose borders we shall never cross.

My Child

When I last saw my child
He only ate porridge.
Now he's sad.

He eats bread and meat with a fork and knife,
And with manners, which already prepare him
To die politely, and quietly.

He thinks that I'm a sailor,
But knows I have no ship.
And that we have no sea.
Only vast distances, and winds.

My father's movements in prayer,
And my own in love
Lie already folded in his small body.

To be grown up is
To bake the bread of longing,
To sit the whole night long
With a reddening face
Opposite the open oven.

My child sees everything.

And that magic-spell 'See you',
Which he's learnt to say,
Is only valid among the dead.

Song of Resignation

1
I resign!

My son has my father's eyes,
My mother's hands,
And my own mouth.
There is no further need of me. Many thanks.
The refrigerator is beginning to hum towards a long
 journey.
An unknown dog sobs over the loss of a stranger.

2
I resign!

I paid my dues to so many funds.
I am fully insured.
Let the world care for me now;
I am knotted and tied with it and all of them.
Every change in my life will cost them cash.
Every movement of mine will hurt them,
My death will dispossess them.
My voice passes with clouds
My hand, stretched out, has turned into paper.
 Yet another contract.
I see the world through the yellow roses
Someone has forgotten
On the table near my window.

3
Bankruptcy!
I declare the whole world to be a womb.

And as of this moment
I appoint myself,
Order myself
At its mercy.
Let it adopt me. Let it care for me.

I declare the President of the United States to be my
    father,
The Chairman of the Soviet Union to be my power of
    attorney,
The British Cabinet to be my family,
And Mao Tse Tung to be my grandmother.

I resign!

I declare the heavens to be God:
They all together go ahead and do those things
That I never believed they would.

To My Mother

1

Like an old windmill
Two hands always raised
To howl at the sky
And two lowered
To make sandwiches.

Her eyes are clean and glitter
Like the Passover eve.

2

At night she will put
All the letters
And the photographs
Side by side.

So she can measure
The length of God's finger.

3

I want to walk in the deep
Wadis between her sobs
I want to stand in the terrible heat
Of her silence.

I want to lean on the
Rough trunks
Of her pain.

4

She laid me,
As Hagar laid Ishmael
Under one of the bushes.

So that she won't have to be at my death
In the war,
Under one of the bushes
In one of the wars.

Mayor

It's sad
To be the Mayor of Jerusalem.
It is terrible.
How can any man be the mayor of a city like that?

What can he do with her?
He will build, and build, and build.

And at night
The stones of the hills round about
Will crawl down
Towards the stone houses,
Like wolves coming
To howl at the dogs
Who have become men's slaves.

My Father Fought Their War
for Four Years

My father fought their war for four years
And he didn't hate his enemies or love them.
But I know, that even there
He formed me daily out of his little calms
So rare; he gathered them out of the bombs
And the smoke,
And he put them in his frayed knapsack
With the last bits of his mother's hardening cake.

And with his eyes he gathered nameless dead,
He gathered many dead on my behalf,
So that I will know them in his look and love them.

And not die, like them, in horror . . .

And he filled his eyes with them in vain:

I go out to all my wars.

The United Nations Command in Jerusalem

The mediators, the peace-makers, the compromisers,
    the pacifiers,
Live in the white house
And receive their nourishment from far away,
Through twisting channels, through dark veins,
    like a foetus.

And their secretaries are lipsticked and laughing,
And their immune chauffeurs wait below, like horses
    in a stable,
And the trees whose shadow shades them, have their
    roots in disputed territory,
And the delusions are children who go out into the
    fields to find cyclamen
And do not come back.

And the thoughts circle above, uneasily, like
    scout-planes,
And they take photographs, and return, and develop
    the film
In dark, sad rooms.

And I know that they have very heavy chandeliers,
And the boy that I was sits on them and swings
In and out, in and out, and out, and does not come
    back.

Later on, the night will bring
Rusty and crooked conclusions out of our ancient lives.

And above all the houses, the music
Will gather all the scattered things
Like a hand gathering crumbs off the table
After the meal, while the talk continues
And the children are already asleep.

And hopes come to me like daring sailors
Like discoverers of continents
To an island
And they rest for a day or two,
And then they sail away.

You Also Were So Tired

You also were so tired of being an advertisement for
The world, for the angels to admire: It's lovely here.
Take a rest from smiling. And without complaint,
Let the sea wind pleat your mouth.

You won't mind, like flying paper
Your eyes also fly; fruit also dropped off the sycamore
How does one say 'to love' in the language of water,
What are we in the language of earth?

Here is the road and the going on it, what does it
    mean —
Whatsoever hill, the Last Wind. Which prophet . . .
And at night, out of my sleep you speak.
And how shall I answer, and what shall I bring?

Two Bedouin Poems

I
He Lives in a House in the City

Buttons fall away, one by one,
Not in battles, not in rape –
From time to time they jump off in little explosions.
A dry sob of trousers and shirts.

Across the wall a yellow woman
Teaches children to play the guitar and a harmonica.
I provide her
With the dry air, the air longing for harmonicas.

Against my will
The barber cuts off a black straggling hair growing in
    my nose,
Extinguishing the rage,
Castrating the fury
In my nose.

And in the nights
Moonlight pierces through the crack in the
    letter-box,
Lights it,
White
Like a letter.

He Loves

No house would have us.

I stretched myself above you, like a tent,
I spread myself beneath you,
A straw mattress.

Your red dress opened up heavenwards,
Like a goblet –
You sat on me upright
To keep your thighs off the hard ground.

'Madman,' you said in your strange language.

His dog died in his chains.
His friends remote –
His son dreams the saying of Kaddish.

Indian Summer in Princeton

Indian summer is a Jewish summer.
Your eyes are so heavy they almost fall out –
Held back, they are, by the sadness of your face.
They do not fall out because of dryness,
And the forgetting of the fruit,
But because of the weight of the remembering.
The ground beneath us moves further away –
This falling away will go on,
And go on.

It was Sunday, their Sabbath,
Time to sit down and ask ourselves
Whom we really love.
In the house lives someone whose name is not the
     same as the name on the gate –
A woman told me that she does not love her life
And which of the trees are sick, just as people are sick.

But in my dreams I look at bright, blinding
     Jerusalem –
And that's why Jerusalem's black now,
Like an under-exposed photograph.

The Heart Is a Corrupt Director[*]

The last days of summer
Are the last days of two, together.

The heart is a corrupt director.

Departing departs from departing.
And in the nights it is written:
Despair which despaired of us
Became hope.

I think that even Newton discovered
Whatever he discovered
In the lull between
One pain and another.

What bearing could this have
On the headiness of our lives?
What bearing on the soft talk
Which surrounds them?
What manner of things have to fall
From which tree, for us to learn?

It is terrible to battle against love
With sleeping pills. What have we come to!

[*]Theatrical director.

National Thoughts

You: trapped in the homeland of the Chosen People.
On your head a cossack's fur hat,
Child of their pogroms.
'After these words.' Always.
Or, for instance, your face: slanting eyes,
Pogrom-Year eyes. Your cheekbones, high,
Hetman's cheekbones, Hetman the rabble-king.
Hassid dancing, dutiful, you, naked on a rock in the
    early evening by the canopies of water at
    Ein Geddi
With eyes closed and your body open like hair.

After these words, 'Always.'
Every day I know the miracle of
Jesus walking upon the waters,
I walk through my life without drowning.

To speak, now, in this tired language
Torn from its sleep in the Bible –
Blinded, it lurches from mouth to mouth –
The language which described God and the Miracles,
Says:
Motor car, bomb, God.

The squared letters wanted to stay closed,
Every letter a locked house,
To stay and to sleep in it for ever.

If I Forget Thee, Jerusalem

If I forget thee, Jerusalem,
Then let my right be forgotten,
Let my right be forgotten, and my left remember.
Let my left remember, and your right close
And your mouth open near the gate.

I shall remember Jerusalem
And forget the forest – my love will remember,
Will open her hair, will close my window,
Will forget my right,
Will forget my left,

If the west wind does not come
I'll never forgive the walls
Nor the sea, nor myself.
Should my right forget
My left shall forgive,
I shall forget all water,
I shall forget my mother.

If I forget thee, Jerusalem,
Let my blood be forgotten.
I shall touch your forehead,
Forget my own,
My voice change
For the second and last time
To the most terrible of voices –
Or silence.

Rain on a Battlefield

It rains on my friends' faces,
On my live friends' faces,
Those who cover their heads with a blanket.
And it rains on my dead friends' faces,
Those who are covered by nothing.

The First Battles

The first battles raised
Terrible love-flowers
With near-killing kisses
Like shells.
The boy soldiers
Are driven in our city's handsome buses:
Number 12, number 8 and number 5 go to the front.

High-Heeled Shoes

The earth answered several times:
Come in!
When you crossed the road in your tapping
High-heeled shoes,
It said, Come in!
But you couldn't hear.

They Call Me

Taxis below
And angels above
Are impatient.
At one and the same time
They call me
With a terrible voice.

I'm coming, I am
Coming,
I'm coming down,
I'm coming up!

It's a Long Time Since
Anybody's Asked

It's a long time since anybody's asked
Who lived in these houses, and who last spoke; who
Forgot his overcoat in these houses,
And who stayed. (Why didn't he run away?)

A dead tree stands amongst the blossoming trees.
   A dead tree.
It's an old mistake, never understood,
And at the edge of the country; the beginning
Of somebody else's time. A little silence.
And the ravings of the body and hell.
And the end of the end which moves in whispers.
The wind passed through this place
And a serious dog watched humans laugh.

Translated by Harold Schimmel

The Bull Comes Home

The bull comes home from his workday in the ring
After drinking coffee with his fighters
And leaving them a note with his exact address
And the place of the red handkerchief.
(The sword stays stuck in his stiff-necked neck.
   And it stays.)
And that he's at home now
And sitting on his bed, with his heavy
Jewish eyes. He knows
It hurts the sword too, when it plunges into flesh.
In the next reincarnation he'll be a sword:
The hurt will stay.
("The door
Is open. If not, the key is under the mat.')
He knows the mercy of evening
And true mercy. In the Bible
He is listed with the clean animals.
He is very kosher, chews his cud
And even his heart's divided and cleft
Like a hoof.
Out through his breast break hairs
Dry and grey as from a split mattress.

During Our Love Houses Were Completed

During our love houses were completed
And someone, beginning then,
Learned to play the flute. His études
Rise and fall. You can hear them
Now when we no longer fill each other
As birds fill a tree,
And you change coins, compulsively,
From country to country,
From urge to urge.

And even though we acted madly,
Now it seems we didn't swerve much
From the norm, didn't disturb
The world, its people and their sleep.
But now it's over.

Soon
Of us two there won't be left either
To forget the other.

Situation

Easy dress for the easy life.
Shirt over belt,
As my face already gets heavy
And my clothes scattered and vulnerable:
Unclosed clothes.

Who lives in those houses?
A stranger lives there. A gurgle lives
And gargles.
The palms of my feet like ancient parchment
With the script of my going.
I have rubber soles. Who's for me?
Rubber's for my feet for the easy
Leaps.

I'm a hero. I'm not afraid.
And to stop fearing is to stop loving.

May your enemies be lost, little by little,
Your loves lost. Amen.

End of Summer Evening in Motsa

A lone bulldozer fights with his hill
Like a poet, like all who work here alone.
A heavy lust of ripe figs
Pulls the evening's ceiling to the level of the earth.
Fire has already eaten the thorns
And death won't have to do a thing except
Fold up like disappointed flames.
I can be consoled: a great love
Can also be a love for landscape.
A deep love for wells, a burning for olive-trees,
Or digging like bulldozers alone.

My thoughts are always polishing my childhood
Till it's become like a hard diamond,
Unbreakable, to cut
Into the cheap glass of my maturity.

Spy

Many years ago
I was sent
To spy out the land
Beyond the age of thirty.

And I stayed there
And didn't go back to my senders,
So as not to be made
To tell
About this land

And made
To lie.

Hike with a Woman

When after hours of walking
You discover suddenly
That the body of the woman stepping beside you
Wasn't meant
For travel and war,

And that her thighs have become heavy
And her buttocks move like a tired flock,
You swell with a great joy
For the world
In which women are like that.

I Am Big and Fat

I am big and fat.
Against every kilo of fat,
Was added a kilo of sadness.

I was a great stutterer, but since
I learned to lie, my speech pours out like water.
Only my face stayed heavy
Like syllables impossible to pronounce,
Stumble-stones, stammering.

Sometimes my eyes still show flashes
Like fire from remote guns
Very far inside me. Old battle.

I demand of others
Not to forget. Myself, only to forget.

In the end, forgotten.

We Did It

We did it in front of the mirror
And in the light. We did it in darkness,
In water, and in the high grass.

We did it in honour of man
And in honour of beast and in honour of God.
But they didn't want to know about us,
They'd already seen our sort.

We did it with imagination and colours,
With confusion of reddish hair and brown
And with difficult gladdening
Exercises. We did it
Like wheels and holy creatures
And with chariot-feats of prophets.
We did it six wings
And six legs

But the heavens
Were hard above us
Like the earth of the summer beneath.

Achziv Poems

1

Broken by the sea,
My head a broken tin.
Sea water fills it
And drains out.

Broken by the sea.
A dirge my lament,
Froth on the lips of the cliffs.
The sea has rabies
Has sea sickness
More dog than dog
More sea than all seas.

Broken by the sea
My lament.

2

Old millstones separated
And laid out for show
At the two ends of the village.
From great longing
They continue to grind between them
Lover's time.

Naked people in the sand talk about
Political problems. It's absurd!
Little piles of clothes in the distance.
Birds cry from an island. Pink buttocks
And muscles like sleeping fish. It's

Absurd even to ask 'what's the time'
When you're naked. A white stripe on your wrist.
Better, dialogue:
'Di-', she said. 'alogue', he said,
Di-, di-, di-, alogue, alogue.

Our friend hid his typewriter
In the broom-bush. Camouflaged in the branches.
Tak, tak, di-, di-, di-, alogue.

3
All night you lay awake on your back.
There was another wind
And there was a wind like you.
The light of the moon
Threw on the wall
One more lattice.
'The key's under the stone near the gate.'
In the morning the outline of your body appeared
Marked by cigarette butts
On the floor.

4
Your green eyes were
Blue for my brown eyes
After this night.

And wrinkles appeared on the sheets:
No, not from age.

5
Around the dead word 'we-loved'
Covered over by seaweed in the sand,
The curious mob crowded.

And until evening we heard the testimonies
Of waves, one by one,
How it happened.

6

Much waves, much eyes,
Much affliction, much salt,
Much sleep, much deceit,
Much sadness, song in the nights, much
Shells, much sand, the profane, everything.

The explanation – to go on living.
What is our life: so many centimetres of
Distraction and tenderness meat
Between the hard skeleton inside
And the hard air outside.

7

My friend saw horses bathing
In the sea at Akko. He saw them and I feel
Them galloping. What did we look for
In the sand that Tuesday and Wednesday,
What did we look for?
With a little breath I put out your right ear.
With a little breath I put out your left ear.
With little breaths on both your ears
I lit your lusts. A great
Invasion began within us. Our writhing and
Twining bodies were witnesses to the greatness of
    the tussle.
In vain.

8

Tie your weeping with a chain
And be inside with me.

In the partly ruined house
The light lives by himself.
From the darkness they make delicate silverware
For the last meal.

My fish mouth mouth
And your fish mouth nipple
Are attached at night.

After that was a moonlit night
Whiter than Atonement Day.
Your weeping burst the chain.
Fled.

9
In the sand we were two-headed Cerberus
With bared teeth. In the afternoon
Your one leg was in the east and your second in the
    west
And I in the middle, leaning on my forelegs,
Looking to the sides with suspicion, roaring awfully,
Lest they take my prey from me.

Who are you?
A poor Jewish kid from the diaspora
Skullcap on the head. From there. From that time.

All night we're together. No
Heavy memories, sticky feelings. Just
Muscles, tensing and relaxing.

In another continent of time,
The dead Rabbis of my childhood appear,
Holding the gravestones high over

Their heads.
Bound up in the knot of my life.

My God, my God,
Why have you not forsaken me!?

10

With the daring glance of Columbus
I look out between towels hung
In the window. The sun sets
In a red dress.
Four boats pass from evening
To evening from behind a handkerchief.
Salt in the little salt cellar on the table,
And outside all the salt in the world.

Seven crumpled panties
Around your bed, for the seven
Days we were here.
Seven withered roses
In seven colours.

11

A one-piece bathing suit:
The big voice of the mob.
A crazy somersault.
The applause of my hand on your body,
Wild applause.

The dry element and the
Moist in a great longing
Destroy each other.

Hesitating veins.

Blue trying to look pink.
I live by your ankles.
My member stands up with solemn ceremony
As if to listen.

I'll leave you beside the sea
Until your reddish hair goes green,
Until my black briefcase is buried in weeds
Like a long-sunk ship.
I'll whip cries out of you,
To make up for all the silences.
Heady revenge.
God.

12

I learned
To relate to your cunt
As to a face.

I speak its former language.
Wrinkled, and made of substance older
Than all remembered ages, written on a book.

It relates to us
As distant offspring,
Playing.

13

A last night near the window,
Outside and in. Hours pass, seven,
Nine, ten.   Eleventh hour:
Moonlight
Turned our bodies into surgical instruments
Hard and gleaming with evil.

Another hour, hours, one, two, three,
Five: in the first light of dawn
Your body was seen caught in the network
Of its nerves, like a sheet
That fell during the night and held,
Stuck in the branches of the dead tree
Before the window.

14

What's it like to be a woman?
What's it like to feel
Vacancy between legs and curiosity
Under the skirt, in summer, in wind,
And chutzpa* at the haunches?

A male has to live with that odd sack
Between his legs. 'Where would you like
Me to put it?' asked the tailor
Measuring my pants
And didn't smile.

What's it like to have a whole voice,
That never broke?
To dress and undress   slitherly
Slinkily   caressively
Like wearing olive oil,
To anoint the body with lithe fabrics,
A silky something,
A murmuring nothing of peach or mauve?
A male dresses with crude gestures of
Buckling and edgy undoing,
Angles, bones and stabs in the air,
And the wind's entangled in his eyebrows.

*Chutzpa: unmitigated effrontery or impudence (Yiddish). (*The Random House Dictionary of the English Language*).

What's it like to 'feel a woman'?
And your body dreams you.
What's it like to love me?

Leavings of a woman on my body,
And signs of the male on yours
Augur the hell
Which awaits us
And our mutual death.

15

If longings start – longings
To be among these houses near this sea,
We'll already be far from them.

My heart's keeners began
Too soon, while I'm still here,
To lament and pluck at my blood and at the sea's sand
And weeds; to beat with fists on cliff,
On sand and on your breasts.

The sea retreats from my face.
My face is the floor of the sea: dry
With cracks and rocks and savage winds.
I grew up like that,
The memories of the soft, green sea still on my face.

16

After these days, I still don't know much
About you. The palm remains bent to the east
Even with no wind from the west. A white boat
Passes parallel to the coast, hard
And clear like God's fingers. The last will
I write in Achziv, in the sand,

Is different from the one I wrote in Jerusalem.
Children's voices buried beneath layers
On the hill reach us in this century
At this hour of the afternoon. They haven't
Stopped playing.

The white, licked beam will never return
And be in a ship, the milled gravel
Can never become a rock. It tears at
My heart, as it tore at the prophets'; with a sharp
Tearing pain a man's turned into a prophet.
It's a good landscape for forgetting and prophecy.
From now on we'll look for windows with other
Views. We'll wander from window to window,
From arch to arch.

Soon the abandoned ship's anchor will be
Decoration for houses and yards. Our hearts too
Will be just an amulet,
Hung inside in dreams and blood.

from *The Journey of the Last Benjamin of Tudela*

I am a man approaching his end.
What seems like youthfulness in me, is not
Youthfulness, but madness,
Because only death can halt this madness.
And what seems like deep roots I put down,
Is nothing but entanglement on
The surface: spastic knots and cramp of grasping hands,
Jumbled ropes and mania of chains.

I am a man alone. I am not a democracy.
The executive, the loving and the legislative power
In one body. The eating, gluttonous, and the vomiting
    power,
The hating power and power of hurting
Blind power and mute power.
I was not elected. I am a demonstration, I carry
My face like a slogan. It's all written there. Everything.
Please, no need to use tear gas,
I already weep. No need to disperse me,
I am dispersed,
And the dead, too, are a demonstration.
When I visit my father's grave, I see
The tombstones carried high in the hands
Of the dust beneath:
They're a mass demonstration.

. . . .

I think of forgetting as of a slowly ripening fruit,
Which once ripe will never be eaten, because it won't be

And won't be remembered:
Its ripeness is its forgetting. When I lay
On my back my bones fill
With a sweetness
Of my little son's breath.
He breathes the same air as me,
Sees the same sights,
Yet my breath is bitter and his breath is sweet
Like rest in the bones of the tired.
The memory of my childhood be blessed: his
    childhood.

Jews in the Land of Israel

We forget where we came from. Our Jewish
Names from the exile reveal us,
Bring up the memory of flower and fruit, medieval
    cities,
Metals, knights that became stone, roses mostly,
Spices whose smells dispersed, precious stones,
    much red,
Trades gone from the world.
(The hands, gone too.)

The circumcision does it to us,
Like in the Bible story of Shechem and the sons
    of Jacob,
With pain all our life.

What are we doing here on our return with this pain.
The Longings dried up with the swampland,
The desert flowers for us and our children are lovely.
Even fragments of ships, that sunk on the way,
Reached this shore,
Even winds reached. Not all the sails.

What are we doing
In this dark land that casts
Yellow shadows, cutting at the eyes.
(Sometimes, one says even after forty
Years or fifty: 'The sun is killing me.')

What are we doing with souls of mist, with the names,
With forest eyes, with our lovely children, with
    swift blood?

Spilt blood isn't roots of trees,
But it's the closest to them
That man has.

A Song of Praise to the Lovely Couple Varda and Schimmel

Jerusalem in the week of the marriage of
Schimmel: I saw a foreign beatnik shoulder
His wrapped guitar like a rifle.
I saw a beggar put out a jingling hand
At the entrance to the public pissoir across from
Buttoning men. And in the Russian Compound
I heard at night fresh whores
Who sang and danced in jail:
Esty, Esty, Esty, take me.

Jerusalem sunk in audio-visual love
Jerusalem still drunk
Froth of tourists on her lips.

I take her temperature:
38 degrees in the shade of her armpits.
100 degrees of joy
In the mouth of the gold ring.*

But Motsa!
Schimmel is preparing Motsa for his marriage
From the East 7 red bulldozers
Cut the mountain like a great wedding cake.
10 yellow cement-mixers, 30 workers
With flags and undershirts of phosphorescent orange.
21 explosions in the afternoon:
Mazel Tov!

* 'the mouth of the . . . ring', asshole, in Hebrew.

94

Schimmel and Varda are already descending slowly
In the parachute of the white synagogue.
Now they're standing silent, wrapped
In the cellophane-paper of God's mercy.

Love in one, clean room,
Like a dream of years of good living
Compressed in one minute of sleep.
Schimmel and Varda:

Two tranquillizer pills
Melting slowly
In the mouth of the excited and crumbling world.

Jerusalem, Port City

Jerusalem port city on the shores of eternity.
The Holy Mount is a huge ship, a luxurious pleasure
Liner. From the portholes of her Western Wall happy
Saints look out, travellers. Chassidim on the dock wave
Goodbye, shout hurrah till we meet again. She's
Always arriving, always sailing. And the gates and
    the docks
And the policemen and the flags and the high masts of
    churches
And mosques and the smokestacks of synagogues and
    the boats
Of praise and waves of mountains. The sound of the
    ram's horn is heard: still
Another sailed. Day of Atonement sailors in white
    uniforms
Climb among ladders and ropes of seasoned prayers.

And the trade and the gates and the gold domes:
Jerusalem is the Venice of God.